Franz Wright

# LEAVE ME HIDDEN

*Poems*

Marick Press
*Grosse Pointe Farms, Michigan*

*for Elizabeth*

Where are you from?
*There.*

Where are you headed?
*There.*

What are you doing here?
*Grieving*

— *Rabi'a al-Adawiyya*

## Pass

I left that vast bed
I had been sharing
with madness's other
most frequent fliers, and
through one locked ward
after another I
passed—
at crack of doom, at
(gentian) dawn
I left.

Let the critic smile
and lift his right hind leg

again, I left.
And that
was that—
       I must have died
or something, near

the end of a sad dream
of home, or

was it one
that featured crushing
and irreversible shame?

One of eyes' sentient
rays, beloved eyes
remembered, voices
remembered.
Or one

of strange brothers
reunited at last
on somebody's bookshelf—maybe
one all about how to tell,
when you look back, your
being lifted up from
your annihilation. Or

one of the love that was
going to give back all
the time lost
for its sake. Of

the planet so alone in timeless night.

## Learning to Read

If I had to look up every fifth or sixth word
so what. I looked them up.
I had nowhere important to be.

My father was unavailable, and my mother
looked like she was about to break,
and not into blossom, every time I spoke.

My favorite was the Iliad. True,
I had trouble pronouncing the names,
but when was I going to pronounce them, and

to whom?
My stepfather maybe?
Number one, he could barely speak English;

two, he had sufficient cause
to smirk or knock me down
without any prompting from me.

Loneliness boredom and terror
my motivation
fiercely fueled.

I get down on my knees and thank God for them.

Du Fu, the Psalms, Whitman, Rilke.
Life has taught me
to understand books.

## The World

Forget the world and then forget
that word.

From things about to disappear
be one who turned away in time.

The instrument can't hear
the music.

And the music cannot change
a thing.

Change your heart, that is
sufficiently improbable—

Change your heart and do your little time.

## In Lieu of Rent

The infinite housed in the particular.

(Has it come back, the blizzard we two watched?)

All that must remain unsaid to be expressed.

(Then everything that ought to be said, for example: there is nothing more anachronistic than the avant-garde, all it produces is literature!)

The eternal this very hour, that was its job;

one-room apartments made ghastly in a week, a whole life like an ill-fitting shoe, and

the manuscript on the bird imagery in Chandler unfinishable now—

The old mad haunted head that couldn't.

A lifetime of nostalgia for its most disastrous days, that was its job.

Its little alcoholocaust.

## One

Bodies are endless, but sentience
gazing from endlessly various eyes
is one, and I can prove it.

Music's an idealized and
disembodied nervous system.
Who's the sacrificial famous person now?

The angel of death is the angel of birth.
Look, look, the monster
has tears in his eyes.

A pair of dark glasses
smoking a cigarette;
a pair of dark glasses, initially

and solely manufactured
for ancient Chinese
judges.

When you die the world
is going to die, the world
and all the stars—

what dies when you are born?

When you have to take it to feel, more or less,
the way you once felt
when you weren't taking it,

I'll meet you at high moon.

I'll greet you,
like the other
last speaker of a language.

At the trial of sleep,

theoretically,
I'll be seeing you.
In the aisles of the pharmacy

open all night I'll be waiting.

At the front door of the insane
asylum doll house of your childhood
I'll be waiting, I will meet you

at the marriage of never happen
and forever, I will be you;
at the velvet heartshaped dark

green morning glory leaves, my
dragonfly, sister, sexlessly wed
to me by unbreakable vow,

by corpselike refusal to speak.

## Don't Leave Your Elegy to Somebody Else

Woke up, as always, like an elderly lion deranged by a toothache.

Showered, dressed, and commenced to rehearse

being himself for one entire hour (and failing miserably as usual).

Having the previous evening conclusively proved that the heart
                 can't be constantly redlining. No,
                 not at this late date.

At least he used his powers weird for good (mostly), you can say
                 that for him.

Despite fairly convincing appearances

he loved the truth, the sun.

Dying he didn't take so well, that having to pass through black
                 gates of psychosis once more—

afterwards, though, he was fine (it turns out

he was just low about a quart of Dilaudid), when

over the abruptly windless waters Christ came walking.

He's now the silver winter light it was his job to love:

someday, when it comes again, you'll see.

# T. S. E.

*The golden vision reappears*

Summer lightning, soundless—
like lit-up sky above a warred-on
city at this very moment or
the distant past, just beyond
the horizon. In Maine
today at dawn the little girl
of an old love took me hunting
wild strawberries. Summer
lightning, soundless, and after many years
some words of yours came back:
a happiness all at once
turning to fear, a shining
blindness all around me; but
why? And why now? And how strange
to picture you writing them down
when you have never read them,
will never read them. Lone sail
off Cape Ann barely visible, lost
beyond overcast waters blown white, the lit-inwardly
sapphire and murderous waves, and it's you
about one hundred years ago. You
as a boy, I think. Yes, I say it is.

## ANNUNCIATION

Then let it be done, said
the girl to the blinding
visitor, according to
your word. What else
are you going to say

right hand held out
as if to
ward off a blow.

So
the Word became flesh

for nine human months. Then
with her still-childlike
body,

she uttered it.

# The Poem (2)

Mrs. Alone is always home;
but don't try to phone
Mrs. Alone,

Mrs. Alone
isn't answering the phone.
She is writing her poem,

just leave her alone:
the words may still come,
startling her awake like a phone

ringing in the night. Why
she might even try scribbling them down,
if she can somehow overcome

the fear, its deafening dial tone
in her ear where she lies
dressed in night listening, listening.

## Leave Me Hidden

I was having trouble deciding
which to watch: *Night
of the Living Bloggers,* or
*Attack of the Neck-Brace People.*
In the end I just went for a walk.

In the woods I stopped wondering why
of all trees
this one: my hand
pressed to fissures
and ridges of

bark's hugely magnified
fingerprint, forehead
resting against it
finally, feeling
distinctly

a heartbeat, vast, silently
booming there deep in
my hidden leaves, blessed
motherworld, personal
underworld, thank you

thank you.

# Moon

The moon's a dead rock,
though I still like the word
moon so black in its white space.

Gaze of the unseeable; Bible-
black hair and the long
lampless waters, the vertical stare at

the pilot on the East River drinking his coffee,
the guy doing lines of cocaine
in the snowplow through the night hours—

Fellow night workers, what can we say
to the moon except
"*You* again?"

You again. Little Miss Skull, ghastly prop;
face of a child pretending to sleep,
in a far country.

# Maybe Tomorrow

The spilled blood went on
flowing in my veins,
for the time being. Words

continued to provide me
with a life
while ruining mine—

On TV the same giggling
soft porn stars reporting
the day's major news:

of inflicting pain nobody tired.

Christ did not return,
not as child, not as fire.

## Fayetteville Elegy

So ours is the other, the invisible world now
to you.
Early leaves blowing spreading green

flames.
How strange it all looks—
my room looks different, and I am afraid of it.

A double-barreled blast of 40 mg per nostril later
the universe has turned into a word, the morning light
a look of love. The white rose glows there

on the glass tabletop, filling the room
with the scent of some far away, close to
inaudible voices: the voices of children

issue from whorled earlike depths
as from a fading phone connection.
What can I do but walk toward it?

I cross the room for several years, with grace
and ease I never knew, sidestepping just in time
the avalanche you'll-pay-for-this, resisting

at a star-filled canyon's lip attempting
flight, at last arriving at the bed,
lying down and like you entertaining no need

to rise again, to move my hand, or write
a single word.
Ever.

# The Grape Arbor

I don't so much absent myself
as I am *absented* (and worse,
there's no way to say it), only to wake here
once more on this planet all prison,
population: one. I step outside

and there it is: of each place I will never
again see your face, hear your voice, in the snow
these gray bare strangled grape veins.
Within whose rustling shade, returned,
I still watch you standing, unaware of me

at this remove in time, and smiling
and practically moving your lips, sideways snow
picking up now;
this brown slashing tangle
of crown and gigantic dead bird's nest,

site of a horror emanating out
into the world, then all of space.
The real world, where the first stone
*is* cast; and the others,
oh the others follow soon.

## Torn From a Notebook

I remember buying a Dexter Gorden CD in downtown Boston—
 I wanted to hear him one more time, and be killed by his great
 big gold axe.

This was the first time I had been out of my apartment in over a year.

Clearly I made it home, I put the music on, I remember

saying to myself: this is something I really would have enjoyed.

I couldn't feel a thing except the horror of feeling nothing, and

it seemed so dark out. And that was strange, I could *see* that a
 brightness was there: it was just that I had somehow been
 replaced

by this crushed entity who could endure neither the presence nor
 the absence of light,

who was tortured every second by the memory of being happy,

by finding that he evidently feared and hated everything I'd ever
 cared about, when we shared one heart, while I was still alive.

# Unfinishables

1. *The Strangers*

Caducean
their limbs
entwining,
wielded
though
by what
and to what
purpose, neither
knew (name me
someone who
knows).

2. *Dreamt Words*

Rodent doll,
we begin
to affix the
black petals
to its feet and
little hands.

3. *Stepfather*

I still wake in rage,
all these years
later, a lust
to crack the big heavy bald egg of your skull
against the wall,
exulting—

and so you live on.

4. *Parent*

His one sentence
postcards, could
they be delivered, would
all read *The blizzard I
visit disguised as will
never arrive and
will never be
over.*


5. *Contagion*

I am gimp, I am misspell.
I am *Kind,*
I am *kränkliches Lächeln.*

Don't touch me, I am drown.

Am room of
never
leave—


6. *The World of Men*

Faceless each in his mask made of mirror,
in his armor of mirror.


7. *Medicine Cabinet*

Late at night I am awakened
to take my body to the bathroom.
There I will feed it two or three pills,

*if* it is in actual pain; if
the road leading back to its life
is looking something like an open wound
being slowly unbandaged—
When sadly the good hours have ceased
to outnumber the evil, I
take it by the arm.


8. *On a Poetic Fashion of the Late Twentieth Century*

No more gratuitious non sequiturs,
you said, no more

smirking ironies;
no more claustrophobic

obscurities for obscurity's sake: *No
more,* oh

little future
hank of blonde-haired

skull, from solitary—
yours

to mine—our tapped out
code . . .

9. *Parousia*

*John 12: 9–10*

Day
when all the
dead come forth
not just the one
poor guy
who's only going to die again anyway.

Man,
a white light where the face should go,

*when?*

When.


10. *Divided World*

World divided
into faces that
say something irreparable
has occurred, and
the ones
that soon will.


11. *Odd Numbers*

Unfathomable fate
that sentenced my father
and mother to
marriage, then
*me.*

Although
to be fair, and
speaking in the name
of adolescents
everywhere
(including Milton's
Satan):


refresh, will you,
faltering
memory:

at what point
did I ask to be
born?


12. *Momentum*

Day before the final snow;
pigeon with one crippled foot
who lands on the bench,
sidles over and looks
right into my eyes.
Waiting alertly in the park
for X, who doesn't show.

## The War

*I cannot promise you happiness in this world:*

Mary
to child Bernadette in her vision.

What I can promise you is this
won't go on forever:
oncology pediatrician
to extremely small
patient
haggard with torment.

What was it that little girl
grieving her father's
death said:

I love to lie down on his side of the bed—

put that
in your syringe and
smoke it.

She'll take your hand
and guide you to
the wide white room winter, and

she doesn't need to hear about
what you do not believe.

See, it was a winter war: a Trakl
madhouse,
and

the war is coming back.

But everyone knows that.

Children not yet born will draw it
from inside barbed wire,
lunged at by dogs.

One of them will take your hand and
say I can't promise
you will not suffer
that same
arctic light,
this freezing wind
in your face

when you have no face.

## Someday

Hour of the first snow
circumferenceless;

text
that has suffered so much

in transmission,
this body

which slept
for a time, then

drove around
in dour November

light
that causes everything

to look like
places in the past.

Hour of the first
or was it the last light—

hard to tell
the difference now. I drove

right by my old friend Annie
carrying the cross of her insanity

down Main Street
in the silver sun

unnoticed,
just as I was

attempting to pray,
while groping around

for my lost phone
faintly ringing somewhere

like a far off tolling
no one else can hear: it called

to mind a not so
distant future

tolling
that will be

quite audible
to everyone but me.

## Shopping For A Grave

It is a close and narrow place, eternity, illegible
library of stones with small rabbits

peering out from between them;
there might be a hundred

balding horizontal doors into the earth. Down
there, my very room, its failing light. The

way it looked before I entered, took my place,
picked up a pen. I had to. From life

I found no other refuge: from
myself, my own mind, so close

and lightless, let me live again
and this time try to get it right!

But there is no other life, no place
except the same cramped room where

I have been sitting forever, bolt upright
in a chair, long dead, and dreaming lie amazed.

## On My Father's 80th Birthday

This grave, green book in no known tongue

this door

back to pre-metaphor,

the pre-correspondence.

Wysteria rain where is your child-mother?

If you liked being born you'll love dying.

This is the kind of thing we had to listen to all day

and half the night, the aloners. The waking
'

and sleeping, the speechless and speaking

ones we alternate between, instantaneous

voyagers...

But truly to concentrate, and utterly shut out the world, where
   was there ever place safe enough?

                            No
body I can conceive of.

To listen for once, for one completely lucid minute, one

hour outside of time,

one life, to add a couple words to what cannot be said.

And get this, supposedly I am now older than you are.

What a laugh we'd have had over that one.

I ask you for help, sometimes

I even ask you where you are: what am I, twelve?

And this late inexplicable flowering—

what, I sometimes ask myself, would you have made of this; and

*had you lived could it have come?*

And get no answer.

# I Dreamed I Met William Burroughs

I met William Burroughs in a dream.
It was some sort of bohemian farmhouse;
and he was enthroned, small and skeletal,
in a truly gigantic red armchair.

When I asked him how he was, he replied
Well, you know what they say—for best results,
always mock and frighten lobster before boiling.
Franz—I like that name, Franz. Childe Franz

to the dark tower something or other . . . Hey,
got a smoke? And quit worrying so much:
they can't help themselves, they're like abused dogs
and they're going to react to affection and kindness

with uncontrollable savagery. Just tell them,
You're out of my mind, pal. You're out
of my mind. Either that or, I'm out of yours.
That'll keep them brain-chained to their trees.

## Recurring Dream

"Your father passed at three a.m."—
*passed?*
What is it, some sort of exam?

At this point I find myself
walking in the ice storm's
wake, a diamond

and annihilated wood
in West Virginia, at its heart
a single songbird's

skeleton gripping a branch,
the small beak
parted—

The instant of knowing you're dreaming
and the instant of waking
are one.

Thus,
against delusion, we
possess this one defense.

It won't do any good, but
it is ours.

## Reflection

I wear this small fish hook
of crucifix
Look

how it helps
keep the head weighted
down

down with shame, with
the glory
and shame

Right here
it hangs,
near

the heart's
hidden room
where

a table stands
set for me
not

a dark bar
(no more
that pointless horror)

Table
for two: one
invisible host

and the guest
who is anyone
hungering

thirsting and
hungering
and meeting himself

for the first
time, the maggot
waiting

in the mirror
there at
the bottom

of the
drained
chalice—

## Admonitions to Self

You'll wake and wage
your little
page.

No
to the pornography of sadness.

To any special pleading based on madness—

No to all potential instances in which the person you kill and
　　　　　　the person who kills
you are one.

## The Future

*for Kristen*

Someday
you will find it
gone;

one day, I promise,
it will hurt you
no more.

Whatever it is
(a secret,
a horror)

lodged
in the gray flesh
of memory,

gradually
it is changing:
it is

turning, right now, hour
by hour into
the pearl.

## Untitled Poem In Three Parts

1.

One day black signs appear
on the highway
replacing the old ones
put there to mislead you;
the pretense, even,
of guidance
now taken away.
All four doors locked,
the windows immovable,
and you
up to your neck in—what is it, vodka?
No. It's a salt-tasting
water. Of ocean?
Of birth? Not so. It is nothing,
the tears you have wept
just like anyone else,
the waters of grace, except
in your case the tears
shed in the course of what has turned
into this totally unforeseen and
somewhat comical longevity—
Steering and brakes gone,
and the accelerator
appears, I'm afraid, to be stuck
at one hundred miles per hour,
the road straight, mysteriously
empty and straight.
Straight for now.

2.

When I was young (remember
when cuts healed before your eyes?)—
when I was young
it was so simple. The single
commandment, to me,
was quite clear: Go
and take nothing with you.
Don't have fear
regarding sustenance,
what you will wear,
how you will get there, or
where *there* is—
you will be guided.
And give no thought
to what you will say
when you arrive. To those
who reject you, fail to
open their door,
wish no ill; wipe the shit
from your heel and move on.
I wish that I had died when I was young.
I find no peace in anything
but work, now; and when
it is gone, only
terror remains:
a punishment, perhaps,
and I am all for that!
There is no peace but
at the deep center
of the voice and ice, far
from the looks of derision
and blame that wait
behind my eyes. And
unaware of them

I walk up and down
my room as on a stage,
indifferent to the audience
I sense in front and all around me.
Oceanic darkness of faces I can't see
for the light in my eyes. And how
should I know who they are?
Friends I can't locate,
the dead, a small number
of those not yet
born, the
hall mostly vacant.


3. *Waiting for Company*

Look the cold windy green
wind of her
eyes
I suddenly hear myself
saying
to the cat
(unrecorded
let's hope): for
a moment become
the glad bodiless
sentience, the
I
I once aspired to, one
single rose-
illuminated cloud
off to the north, sailing out
a still-daytime
three-quarters moon, the
first snowflakes,
swirling

like the unseeable
particles of which
all things are made,
but why,
I ask you. Why
in the world
were all these things given
if I could never stay? Why
words for them given and
they themselves taken away?
Why to me, from so far, did you call—
did you tap on my window,
my shoulder.
You spoke (it
is hardly the term)
and I left
wherever I lived,
so to speak,
and whoever I
happened to be with—
wife, brother, friend.
All at once you
got in touch
quite unmistakably,
whatever you are.
And as always
I was prepared
to obey, but
why?
Why
was I filled with such love,
when it was the law
that I be alone?

*March 18-March 25*

Acknowledgements

Some of these poems originally appeared in the following journals: *The New Yorker, Prairie Schooner, The Laurel Review, Pebble Lake Review, Comment Magazine (Toronto), Free Verse,* and *Knockout.*

\*

I would like to point out here that the term *alcoholocaust,* which appears at the end of "In Lieu of Rent," was brilliantly coined by Malcom Lowry in a letter to a friend.

F. W.

ISBN: 978-1934851-10-4

Printed in the United States

MARICK PRESS
P.O. Box 36253
Grosse Pointe Farms
Michigan 48236
www.marickpress.com

www.ingramcontent.com/pod-product-compliance
Lightning Source LLC
Chambersburg PA
CBHW020024050426
42450CB00005B/628